Self-Censorship

Self-Censorship

Glenn C. Loury

polity

The right of Glenn C. Loury to be identified as Author of this Work has been asserted in accordance with the UK Copyright, Designs and Patents Act 1988.

First published in 2025 by Polity Press

Polity Press
65 Bridge Street
Cambridge CB2 1UR, UK

Polity Press
111 River Street
Hoboken, NJ 07030, USA

ISBN-13: 978-1-5095-6740-9

A catalogue record for this book is available from the British Library.

Library of Congress Control Number: 2024951854

Typeset in 12.5 on 15pt Adobe Garamond
by Cheshire Typesetting Ltd, Cuddington, Cheshire
Printed and bound in Great Britain by CPI Group (UK) Ltd, Croydon

The publisher has used its best endeavours to ensure that the URLs for external websites referred to in this book are correct and active at the time of going to press. However, the publisher has no responsibility for the websites and can make no guarantee that a site will remain live or that the content is or will remain appropriate.

Every effort has been made to trace all copyright holders, but if any have been overlooked the publisher will be pleased to include any necessary credits in any subsequent reprint or edition.

For further information on Polity, visit our website:
politybooks.com

Contents

Foreword   vii

Self-Censorship in Public Discourse:
A Theory of Political Correctness and
Related Phenomena   1

Afterword: Self-Censorship in a Time of
War   67

Notes   81

References   94

Foreword

Back in the late 1980s, when I first drafted the lecture that would eventually become my essay "Self-Censorship in Public Discourse: A Theory of Political Correctness and Related Phenomena," it seemed to me that debates about political correctness were only the latest iteration of an ancient dilemma, which is this: to speak in public about fraught political issues can be a risky business. What one ought to say, who one ought to say it to, how one ought to say it, or whether one ought to say anything at all – these have been understood to be pivotal philosophical problems since the time of Plato's *Apology*. The debate is certainly even older than that. This was the problem I wanted to address. One could,

I thought, substitute the modern public sphere – the university campus, the television talk show, the newspaper op-ed page, and so on – for the agora of ancient Athens without altering the basic contours of this problem.

I was teaching at Harvard's Kennedy School of Government at the time. My impetus for the essay, in the first instance, was the emergence on college campuses of the formal and tacit speech codes that came to be called "political correctness." However, my inspiration was not limited to domestic affairs. Upheavals in the former Soviet Union and East Germany, in Czechoslovakia, and in other states that were freeing themselves from repressive and dysfunctional communist governments provided a global context for my ruminations. I read stories of neighbors turning in neighbors to the authorities for thought crimes. I saw reports of widespread silence among people of conscience in the face of gross public injustices. All of these led me to wonder how those governments had managed not merely to enforce regimes of legal censorship but to induce regimens of tacit self-censorship that stifled the critical discourse of entire populations.

Citizens in those nations had good reason to fear the state's reprisal, of course. After all, unemployment, imprisonment, and torture weren't unheard of. But I came to think that the problem of self-censorship is much more subtle than that, entailing as it does not only the iron fist of state repression but also the velvet glove of social cooptation. It seemed to me that it was not just fear of government action that kept people quiet. Rather, what lay at the root of things was the inescapability of drawing an inference *ad hominem* – against the person. This, I came to think, was true both abroad, in the communist nations, and, more subtly, at home in the United States, where an individual's right to self-expression without state interference is supposed to be guaranteed by the constitution.

Even here, I thought, there is no such thing as genuinely "free" speech. Speakers who voice opinions that deviate fundamentally from an audience's beliefs could become subjects of costly personal attack, and there is an inexorable logic to such attacks. For, by knowing that a speaker is willing to be heard saying certain things, an audience can be led, through a process of rational inference, to draw negative conclusions about that speaker's motives, loyalties, and character. Listeners may be tempted, consciously or not, to villainize the person rather than to respond to that person's ideas. They may be led to brand their target a "racist," an "extremist," a "misogynist," a "traitor," or some other disreputable social type, concluding that the speaker's views must be disavowed and his presence disdained.

In such an atmosphere, the individual's fear-inspired suppression of his own true beliefs is understandable. But I am at pains to insist that this self-censorship comes with some insidious effects. Challenges to a faltering status quo get shut out of the public discussion. Urgent moral deliberations get reduced to tiresome exercises in expressive etiquette. In the late 1980s, as the political correctness debates raged across college campuses, I watched with dismay while my colleagues, students, and friends – fearing reprisal for talking in ways that violated new and sometimes radical social norms – succumbed to the lure of a quiet conformity. Those who should have known better, I thought, were stifling themselves.

I began to think more deeply about the problem. Several questions occurred to me. What kinds of informal public censure does unpopular speech elicit, and why? How do people counteract the inclination to self-censor? Does this rhetorical reticence distort our public conversation and, if so, how? Do institutions such as the university and the media play a special role in either fostering or countering these adverse effects? The essay I finally published in 1994 tried to address such questions.

I am an economist, not a political theorist, historian, or philosopher, so it may seem strange that I was attracted to an issue that, on its face, has so little to do with things like resource allocation and market inefficiencies. And, true enough, those mathematical models I had drilled into me as a student at Northwestern and MIT a half-century ago are of very little help when trying to understand the sociolinguistics of public speech. But I am not *only* an economist. As a public intellectual of decidedly conservative leanings – and an African American one, no less! – I have experienced the pressure to conform to the language and thought native to the progressive academic and media circles in which I was traveling. I have even succumbed to those pressures on occasion. When I didn't, I found myself receiving admonishments, criticisms, condemnations, and outright insults – as a just recompense for being a Black academic who, by favoring a conservative policy or by opposing a liberal one, disappointed some widely held expectations from my "type." I have always had a personal stake in the study of this issue.

Yet rereading "Self-Censorship in Public Discourse" with thirty years' hindsight, I don't think I can call it a "conservative" or a "liberal" piece of writing, even though I doubt it would have occurred to a contemporary liberal to write it. I wasn't making a partisan argument. Rather I was trying to lay bare the underlying conditions that cause a juridical prohibition on censorship to become a social impossibility. And *that* is a subject about which economics has something to say.

The US government may not punish you for expressing yourself as you see fit, but *truly free speech* – speech that comes at no cost to the speaker – simply does not exist. This is but one version of a first principle any economics undergraduate will recognize: "There's no free lunch." Under ever present conditions of scarcity, every benefit necessarily comes at some cost – whether that be a production cost (someone, somewhere paid for your sandwich) or an opportunity cost (you could have been doing something else instead of eating it). An analogous truism applies to the public speaker, it occurred to me. This is especially so if what the speaker has to say is broadly unpopular and, in consequence, the social cost of having said it is quite high.

Each of us learns this lesson, whether in an economics class or in the world at large. And as I began to test my thesis – there is no such thing as truly free speech – against a variety of examples, both observed and invented, it became clear to me that the penalties levied on acts of unpopular speech most often occur against a background of social conformity. That is, unpopular speech acts are departures from an established convention of expression and opinion. Such deviations come with negative consequences, which could be as modest as an eyeroll or as weighty as sudden unemployment. The question arises as to just how such an equilibrium of conformity sustains itself. That is, how does political correctness, a mode of restrained speech, become self-enforcing? When it does, how do speakers who wish to avoid the penalties incurred by unpopular speech nevertheless communicate their views to receptive audiences? And, when there are diverse audiences, how do the various listeners infer whether a given speaker is "one of us," and thus to be trusted, or "one of them," and thus someone to be viewed with suspicion?

To appreciate the subtlety and sensitivity of these questions, I consulted some works in the social sciences that proved to be of invaluable assistance. I was especially inspired by the preeminent thinkers Erving Goffman, Albert O. Hirschman, and Thomas C. Schelling. Their work, firmly rooted in rigorous social science, is also rendered in exquisitely precise prose that can be understood by a general readership. This essay endeavors to emulate their artistry in this regard.

It should be clear to any reader of "Self-Censorship in Public Discourse" that, as a general matter, I took political correctness to be an undesirable form of repression and coercion. I still hold that view, in the main, for all the same reasons. Nowadays political correctness is seen to be a cultural artifact of the late twentieth century. The term is almost always placed between scare quotes. Yet the sociolinguistic conditions I was analyzing then are no less prevalent now – and their consequences can be even more dire.

In "Self-Censorship in a Time of War," which is the Afterword for this short volume, I consider my own recent experience of self-censorship as a contemporary case study. In belligerent societies, war pushes social contradictions to their extremes. The need for the civic-minded to speak out in spite of the pressure to affirm consensus views may be urgent, but at the same time the adverse consequences of doing so can be quite daunting. My own encounter with this problematic necessity is, admittedly, a rather minor matter when set against all the other costs of war. But it is emblematic of a troubling social mood, which prefers diffident silence to the necessary cacophony of dissent.

Uncertainty about what motivates "senders" of public messages leads "receivers" to read between the lines in order to discern senders' deepest commitments. Anticipating this, senders write between the lines, editing their expressions so as to further their own ends. I examine how this interactive process of inference and deceit affects the quality and extent of public deliberations on sensitive issues. A principal conclusion is that genuine moral discourse on difficult social issues can become impossible when the risks of upsetting some portion of one's audience are too great. Reliance on euphemism and platitude should be expected in this strategic climate. Groups may embark on a tragic course of action that was believed by many, from the outset, to be ill conceived but that has become impossible to criticize.

Self-Censorship in Public Discourse

A Theory of Political Correctness and Related Phenomena *

The great enemy of clear language is insincerity. When there is a gap between one's real and one's declared aims, one turns as it were instinctively to long words and exhausted idioms, like a cuttlefish spurting out ink. Thus political language has to consist largely of euphemism, question-begging and sheer cloudy vagueness.

George Orwell (1968, p. 137)

* Original publication: Loury, Glenn C. 1994. Self-censorship in public discourse: A theory of "political correctness" and related phenomena. *Rationality and Society* 6(4): 428–61. DOI:10.1177/10 43463194006004002.

I

1 Putting the Political Correctness Debate into Perspective

Political correctness is an important theme in the raging culture war that has replaced the struggle over communism as the primary locus of partisan conflict in American intellectual life. Starting on campuses over issues such as abortion, affirmative action, multicultural studies, environmentalism, feminism, and gay rights, the political correctness debate has spread into newsrooms, movie studios, and even the halls of Congress. Critics, mainly on the right, claim that only the "correct" views on these and other sensitive issues can be expressed – on campus, in print, on film, or in electoral politics – without eliciting extreme, stifling reactions from activists who seek to make their opinions into an enforced orthodoxy. They cite a litany of woes about how, in venues where the left is most powerful, those who express even mildly divergent views are treated poorly. In response, liberals describe these charges as over-blown and insist that their efforts to hold people accountable for what they say and write are justified in the name of legitimate moral concerns.

We can usefully distinguish two levels at which the disagreement occurs. At the primary level, partisan arguments on certain questions divide public opinion: How bad is the "date rape" problem and what should be done about it? What texts are canonical, and are nonwestern cultures adequately represented among them? What causes the violence that erupts among young Black men in cities and how can it be reduced? What is the nature and the moral standing of homosexuality? Disagreements on these substantive matters stem from the different values, factual judgments, and theoretical frameworks that people employ to analyze the world around them. Such disagreements are inevitable – and healthy. They have the potential to engender constructive exchanges, from which all participants can learn and better public policies can emerge.

At a secondary level, however, a contentious discussion is taking place over the very nature of these primary-level discussions. Are speakers treated respectfully regardless of the popularity of their views? Are some opinions given privileged access to the media? Are people candid in their arguments? Who can talk about what topics and when, without violating some unspoken canon of decency? Do advocates of one position seek to prevent or to discredit the expression of opposing ideas? Do some arguments so offend the sensibilities of some citizens that they should be preemptively excluded from public debate?

These two levels of debate can become confused. Some complaints about political correctness really are, upon examination, laments that within a certain community of discourse the complainer's views are unpopular. However, the most serious questions raised in the political correctness debate focus on this secondary level. The fundamental issue is whether the climate for the voicing of opinion in important forums (and the universities are by no means the only forums of interest) continues to permit a constructive, informative dialogue on vital matters of common concern. Increasingly, it seems to me, there is reason to doubt that this is so.

Thus I have undertaken in this essay to provide an analysis of political correctness. Unlike many who have written on this topic, I will not waste time telling "horror stories" about the excesses of political correctness zealots, or lamenting their influence on campuses.[1] Instead, I will endeavor to lay bare the underlying logic of political correctness – to expose the social forces that create and sustain movements of this sort. Two preliminary observations will help with setting the stage for my analysis.

First, although political correctness is often spoken of as a threat to free speech on campuses (and this is indeed the case when it results in legal restrictions on open expression, as those imposed by formal speech codes), the more subtle threat is the voluntary limitation on speech that a climate of social conformity encourages. It is not the iron fist of repression, but the velvet glove of seduction that is the real problem. Accordingly, I treat the political correctness phenomenon as *an implicit social convention of restraint on public expression that operates within a given community.* Conventions of this kind can arise because (a) a community needs to assess whether the beliefs of its members are consistent with its collective and formally avowed purposes, and (b) scrutiny of the members' public statements is an often efficient way to determine whether their beliefs cohere with communal norms. This need to police group members' beliefs so as to ferret out deviants, along with the fact that the expression of heretical opinions may be the best available evidence of deviance, creates the possibility for what I call *self-censorship*: members whose beliefs are sound but who nevertheless depart from communal wisdom in some respect are compelled, through fear of ostracism, to avoid the candid expression of their opinions.

Second, despite the attention that has been given to recent developments on campus, the phenomenon of political correctness, understood as an implicit convention about the restrained nature of public speech, is neither new nor unusual. Indeed, pressuring speakers and writers to affirm acceptable beliefs and to suppress unacceptable views is one of the constants of the political experience. All social groups have norms concerning the values and beliefs that are appropriate for their members to hold on the most sensitive issues. Those seen not to share the consensus view may suffer low social esteem and face a variety of sanctions from colleagues: apostates and heretics are unwelcome within the councils of the faithful. In the United States, communists and their sympathizers paid a heavy price for their "incorrect" views during the early Cold War. "Uncle Toms" – Blacks seen as being too eager to win favor with their White overlords – are still treated like pariahs by other Blacks, who greatly value racial solidarity. Jews critical of Israel or Muslims critical of Islam may find that they "can't go home again."

Therefore a theory of contemporary problems around political correctness should be broad enough to address these related phenomena. I sketch here an approach that, I believe, meets this requirement. My theory is based on a conception of political communication that stresses strategic considerations. From this point of view, people engaged in primary-level debates over policy questions must also – at the secondary level, if you will – consider how their interests are affected by the specific manner in which they express themselves. The next section develops the main ideas along this line. This strategic approach is then applied to explain how conformity in public speech emerges as a stable behavioral convention within a given community. Section 4 reviews some historical examples of censored public discussions, and Section 5 discusses some broader implications, for both the style and the substance of policy debates, of the kind of expressive behavior identified here. A special effort is made throughout this discussion to shed light on some of the more problematic features of public rhetoric on race-related issues in the United States.

2 Strategic Behavior in the Forum

George Orwell's skepticism about political rhetoric, elaborated in his essay "Politics and the English Language" (from which I quoted), has much to recommend it. Political communication – the transmission of ideas and information about matters of common concern, with the intention to shape public opinion or affect policy outcomes – is tricky business. Both those sending and those receiving messages must be wary. Senders want to persuade or inform via spoken and written words. They strive to convey their intended message while avoiding misinterpretation or discovery. Receivers want to distill, from incoming rhetoric, information that may be useful for forming an opinion or making a decision; but they want not to be manipulated or deceived. To be effective, both parties need to behave *strategically*. Naive communication – where speakers state literally all that they think, and an audience accepts their representations at face value – is rare and foolish in politics. A political speaker's *expression* is more often a calculated effort to achieve some chosen end; and an audience's *impression* of the speaker is usually arrived at with recognition that this is so.

Recall the oratorical confrontation in Act III, Scene 2 of *Julius Caesar*. Caesar has been murdered by a group of conspirators that includes Brutus. Antony, who is close to Caesar and has no part of the conspiracy, is outraged and bent on revenge. Brutus goes before the crowd to explain his actions, saying that Caesar was ambitious, a man who would be king, who had to be stopped for the sake of the republic. "Not that I loved Caesar less, but that I loved Rome more," he declares, relying on his reputation for honor and decency to sway the crowd. He argues directly; his speech is naive, guileless, literal. He seems to prevail as he takes his leave. Then Antony rises, saying, "Friends, Romans, countrymen, lend me your ears. I come to bury Caesar, not to praise him." This, of course, is not true. He praises Caesar profusely, reminding the audience of Caesar's greatness in war, of his kindness and generosity in peace ("Ambition should be made of sterner stuff!"). Nevertheless, the assembled citizens take Antony at his word. As for his view of Brutus and the others, he does not overtly disparage them; he seems to accept their stated motives: "Brutus says Caesar was ambitious, and Brutus is an honorable man." He never reveals that revenge is his own motive. Yet, by its end, his powerfully manipulative oration has made the words "honorable man," said in reference to Brutus, mean exactly their opposite; and defense of Brutus by anyone in the crowd has become impossible. Shortly after, civil war breaks out. Shakespeare shows us here the potential for political gain that lies in strategic expression, and also the dangers – for an advocate as well as for the public good – of naive behavior in the forum.

I want to explore how the form and substance of collective deliberations on sensitive issues are affected by strategic behavior in the forum. There is always some uncertainty when ideas and information are exchanged between parties that may not have the same objectives. Each message bears interpretation. There is no such thing as a context-free expression. We are inevitably reading and writing "between the lines." Because political rhetoric engages interests, expresses values, conveys intent, and seeks to establish commitment to certain courses of action, the risk of manipulation is particularly great in political argument. When people address us in the forum, we must consider what they will do if they get power; we must decide whether they can be trusted; we must wonder, "what type of person is it who would speak to me in this way?"

Erving Goffman has brilliantly analyzed the dilemmas and complexities of communication in the face of this kind of bilateral calculation.[2] Goffman in effect considers the "game" that gets played between two parties to an interaction as constituting a "sender," who expresses him- or herself in some way, and a "receiver," who takes that expression in and reacts to it, forming an impression of the sender.[3] We might, given the purposes of this essay, think of the sender as a political speaker who participates in public debate and of the receiver as a member of the audience who must form an opinion on some controversial matter. Or the sender might be a professor lecturing on American race relations, and the receiver a minority student drawing conclusions about the professor's sensitivity and commitment. The sender has views or values that are not directly knowable to the receiver but that, if known, would significantly alter the receiver's construction of what I call "the meaning in effect" of any expression.[4]

The sender may want to "signal" – that is, convey credibly, but indirectly – that he holds a certain point of view, or may want to disguise the view that he really holds. Knowing that these possibilities exist, receivers will search each expression for evidence of the sender's true motivations and beliefs. From this perspective, to use Goffman's terminology, each act of political communication is a small *performance*, bearing close interpretation. Its meaning in effect – the impression it gives rise to in the receiver's mind – may depend very much on context, and in particular on what other senders, whose values and beliefs are already known to the audience, have been transmitting.

When speakers choose words intended to elicit a particular response, strategic listeners cannot simply accept the literal content of an expression as its meaning in effect. To take the speaker literally is to behave naively, and thus to risk being deceived. Sophisticated listeners must look behind what is spoken or written, in an effort to discern all that is implied by the act of speaking or writing in a given way.

The sender of a public message intended to shape opinions and influence policy may have ultimate aims that are not apparent to his audience. And yet, because that sender's values, ideals, and intentions will shape the strategy that he adopts in the forum, a proper decoding of the message requires knowledge of the sender's ultimate aims. For this reason, the interpretation of political expression involves, in an essential way, drawing, from the expressive act, inferences about the sender's motives, values, and commitments. *The search for "true" meaning entails judging the character of speakers* – asking whether they really believe what they say and, just as importantly, whether they hold other, unexpressed views, which if known to us would affect our reception of their arguments.

At the same time, being aware that their speech act is subject to such interpretation and wanting to create the desired impression, skillful speakers will structure their message being mindful of the inferences that listeners are inclined to make. They will try to use to their advantage the patterns of inference established within a given community of discourse. They will avoid expressions known to elicit negative judgments or associations, and will deploy others, known to win favor with the audience or to cast them in a positive light. Thus, in the context of political communication, speakers and listeners, writers and readers, all play an "expression game." For any party, the appropriate behavior depends on the strategies that are used by all other players. An *equilibrium* in this game can be thought of as a convention that governs the rhetoric used by senders and the strategies of inference and interpretation employed by receivers, such that each party is content to behave as they do, given the pattern of behaviors adopted by all the others.

Take this essay as a case in point. It is public and political, despite the academic veneer. To address the subject of political correctness at a time when power and authority within the academic community are being contested by parties on either side of that issue is to invite scrutiny of one's arguments – scrutiny exercised by would-be "friends" and "enemies." Combatants from the left and the right will try to assess whether a writer is "for them" or "against them." How an essay like this is read and evaluated, what in it is taken seriously and what is dismissed out of hand depends, for many readers, on where they presume the writer is coming from – what they take his ulterior motives to be. This assessment, in turn, is based not simply upon words on the page but also on whatever else can be learned about the writer's character and commitments.

One way to gain insight into the writer's values is to measure his treatment of certain sensitive themes against the standard set by others, whose values may be known.[5]

It is even possible that some readers, on the strength of what they think they know about my opinions from reading other things I have written or from my general reputation, approach this essay with a strong prior assessment of the "real" purposes of my argument – a neoconservative apology for the status quo, let us say. Knowing that I may be read in this way (which can either aid or damage my credibility, depending on the reader), I will, perhaps unconsciously, edit my writing so as to avoid conveying the "wrong" – that is, unintended, even if accurate – impression. I can pander to the assumed prejudices of my audience, I can denounce them, or I can strive to dispel them; but in any event I ignore them at my peril.

Although this essay is an argument about how we argue in public, the discussion also engages substantive matters of controversy. Because I am particularly interested in the structure of public discussion in the United States on racial issues, I occasionally point to those issues to illustrate general principles developed in the argument. For example, I refer to troubling aspects of the public debate on affirmative action. Some readers may question my motives for using these illustrations, suspecting that my argument about deliberative process is really a disguised argument about substance. They may take my observation that discussion of affirmative action is not always fully candid as an indirect attack on the policy itself. They may impute to me a hidden agenda. This possibility has implications for the form of argument that I should make here, if I want to succeed in communicating my general ideas.

I must tread carefully as I try to express my particular "truth." If you are going to read between the lines, looking for my true meaning, the meaning characteristic of my actual albeit not fully expressed sentiments, then I am determined to write between the lines, avoiding (or embracing) certain code words, choosing carefully my illustrative examples, concealing some of my thinking while exaggerating other sentiments – so as to control the impression I make on my audience. I want to write persuasively, but is that really different from manipulation? You want to be informed, or perhaps entertained, but you certainly want not to be fooled.[6]

3 There Is No (Entirely) Free Speech

From this strategic perspective, a regime of political correctness may be viewed as a stable and self-reproducing pattern of expression and inference within a given community, where receivers impute undesirable qualities to senders who express themselves in an "incorrect" way and, as a result, senders avoid such expressions. To illustrate, if known enemies of progressive ideals regularly make a certain argument, then someone who wants to be seen as standing on the right side of history cannot make a similar argument without the risk of being labeled a "reactionary." In a social environment where there are some real racists, if proponents of diversity insist that Blacks be referred to as African Americans and American Indians as Native Americans, a speaker who eschews that terminological distinction in the course of an otherwise admirable argument about diversity invites the conclusion that he is intolerant of ethnic difference. The more prudent course for such speakers is to use the politically correct terms, even when they prefer not to. In a south Florida enclave where hatred of Castro is universal, to argue that the normalization of relations with Cuba should be studied amounts to announcing that the arguer cares nothing for remaining in good standing with his fellows. And in a nearby precinct where reaction against the Cuban immigration runs high, to question the wisdom of making English the state's official language has a similar meaning in effect.

In economics, Gresham's law holds that bad money tends to drive out good. When two types of currency circulate and one is intrinsically more valuable, people hoard the good money and make purchases with the bad. Soon only the bad money remains in circulation. Similarly, people with extreme views can drive moderates – who want to avoid the reputational devaluation of being taken for zealots – out of a conversation. In effect, moderates "hoard" their opinions. Hence the public discourse on some issues (abortion?) can be more polarized than is the actual distribution of public opinion.

What forces, we should ask, could create and sustain such patterns of inference? Note that in the examples above what might be called, in short, an *ad hominem* impulse – that is, an impulse to infer *ad hominem* (or conclude against the person rather than against the argument) – determines the audience's response. Its question is: "'What type of person would say such a thing?" and not: "Does this argument have merit?" *Ad hominem* reasoning lies at the core of the political correctness phenomenon. A speaker's violation of protocol turns the public's attention away from the worth of the case and toward an inquiry into that speaker's character; and the outcome of the inquiry depends on what is known about the character of others who have spoken in a similar way. When sophisticated speakers are aware of this process of inference, many of them will be reluctant to express themselves in a way that is likely to raise suspicion that their ultimate commitments may not conform with the norms of their community.

Ad hominem inference, though denigrated by the high-minded, is a vitally important defensive tactic in the forum. When discussing matters of collective relevance, knowing where the speaker stands helps us gauge the weight we should give an argument, an opinion, or a factual assertion offered in the debate. If we know that a speaker shares our values, we more readily accept from that person observations that run contrary to our initial sense of things. We are less eager to dismiss his rebuttal of our arguments and more willing to believe facts reported by him that carry unpleasant implications.[7] The reason for all this is that, when we believe that the speakers have goals similar to our own, we are confident that any effort they make to manipulate us is intended to advance ends similar to those we would pursue ourselves.[8] Conversely, speakers with values very different from ours are probably pursuing ends at odds with those that we would choose if we had the same information. The possibility of adverse manipulation makes such people dangerous when allowed to remain among us undetected. Thus, whenever political discourse takes place under conditions of uncertainty about the values of participants, a certain vetting process occurs, in which we cautiously try to learn more about the larger commitments of those who advocate a particular course of action.[9]

If, by the various means available, an individual is discovered not to share in the deepest value commitments of a particular community, the reaction may well be to exclude that person from participation in future deliberations and to disparage him publicly for his deviance. The social ostracism, verbal abuse, extreme disapproval, damage to reputation, and loss of professional opportunity that can occur when one is judged to deviate from some strongly held moral consensus are very unpleasant experiences. When there is broad agreement on what constitutes acceptable and unacceptable opinions, prudent persons will conduct themselves so as to avoid giving gratuitous offense to received orthodoxy. Those who speak in flagrant violation of the conventional wisdom must know the risks they are taking and must therefore be acting in full recognition of the possible consequences. Being sanctioned for the expression of disapproved opinions seldom befalls someone by accident. It is more often the result of freely choosing to say the disapproved thing. It is probable that real deviants within a given community – those who are in fact "incorrect" in their political sensibilities and who do not share the moral consensus of the community on the issues in question – find the prospect of ostracism less distressing than those who, in their heart of hearts, agree with the community view in broad outline, although perhaps not with its every detail.

Crucial to my argument, then, is the following syllogism. Suppose that,

(a) within a given community, the people who are most faithful to communal values are, by and large, also those who want most to remain in good standing with their fellows;

(b) and the practice is well established in this community that those who speak in ways that offend communal values do not remain in good standing. Then,

(c) when a speaker is observed to express him- or herself offensively, the odds are increased that the speaker in question is not really faithful to the communal values, as estimated by a listener otherwise uninformed about this person's views.

That (c) follows from (a) and (b) is a simple consequence of rational inference by listeners, given rational behavior by senders. But this reasoning implies that sanctions against some forms of expressions could become a self-sustaining convention: assuming a positive association between fidelity and sociability, there could easily exist an equilibrium in the communal expression game such that "apostates" are identified by their differential willingness to utter phrases known to be associated with a disapproved belief. For, if it is commonly known that morally suspicious speech invites sanction, and if sanctions cause greater harm to those who really share our values than to those who do not, then the very fact that someone chooses to utter the disapproved phrases suggests (statistically) that the speaker probably does not share in the consensus. Suspicious speech signals deviance because, *once the practice of punishing those who express certain ideas is well established, the only ones who risk ostracism by speaking recklessly are those who place so little value on partaking in our community that they must be presumed not to partake in our dearest common values.*

It is in this sense that I can say: "There is no (entirely) free speech." Anyone speaking out on a controversial matter pays the particular price of having others know that he was willing to speak, under a given set of circumstances, in a certain way. When listeners know that not everyone would be willing to pay that price and, specifically, that "true believers" are less likely than "apostates" to risk incurring the community's wrath, they can make empirically valid inferences about the reckless speakers. Norm-offending speech then conveys more than just literal meanings. Anticipating these inferences and wanting not to be seen as deviant, prudent "true believers" may elect to say nothing that risks offending collective sensitivities. By doing so, they leave the field clear for the "apostates," thereby creating the meaning in effect that norm-offending speech identifies deviant belief. In circumstances of this kind, a climate of self-censorship can become entrenched.[10]

Such self-censorship is the hidden face of political correctness. For every act of aberrant speech seen to be punished by the thought police, there are countless other critical arguments, dissent from received truths, unpleasant factual reports, or nonconformist deviations of thought that go unexpressed or whose expression is distorted, because potential speakers rightly fear the consequences of a candid exposition of their views. As a result, the public discussion of vital issues can become dangerously impoverished, as the following examples illustrate.

4 Examples of Censored Public Discourse

A An Incorrect Discussion of the Holocaust

Let us look briefly at the important case of Philipp Jenninger, once president of the Bundestag (parliament) in the former West German Republic. Jenninger was forced to resign in November 1988 after a speech he gave at a special parliamentary session, which marked the fiftieth anniversary of Kristallnacht – the Night of the Broken Glass. In his speech he gave an account of the events that led up to that infamous night in 1938, when German Jews were set upon, their property destroyed, and their lives taken – a night that many historians mark as the beginning of the Holocaust. An uproar was created by the fact that many in his audience construed Jenninger's brutally frank account of prevailing attitudes among Germans in the 1930s as a disguised defense of National Socialism.[11]

Paradoxically, all agreed that Jenninger had for many years been an opponent of totalitarianism of all stripes, a fierce anti-Nazi, and an arch supporter of Israel. Thus he was an unlikely defender of Nazism. No one accused him of being anti-Semitic. However, even before his speech had ended, there were demonstrations of anger from some in the audience who, finding his words profoundly offensive, rushed ashen-faced from the chamber. Yet virtually all reviewers who examined the speech concluded that Jenninger had said nothing untrue, malicious, or defamatory; he simply said things that some people did not want to hear, and did so in a manner that they were unwilling to accept. The context of his remarks and, perhaps more importantly, the voice in which he delivered a part of the speech made his utterances impossible for many Germans to accept. According to one analyst, his mistake was that he had such confidence in his reputation as a friend of Jews and of Israel that he believed he did not need to use the subjunctive mood, or some other grammatical distancing device, when making what would otherwise be perceived as noxious statements.[12]

Jenninger began with a forthright condemnation of Nazi violence:

What took place 50 years ago today in Germany had not been seen in any civilized country since the Middle Ages. ... The violence ... was a measure planned, instigated and promoted by the government. ... The German people remained largely passive. ...

Everyone saw what was happening but most people looked the other way and remained silent.

But he was equally direct in conveying the positive perception that most Germans had of Nazi leadership. At one point Jenninger imagined, as though he were thinking out loud, how a typical German citizen must have viewed the political successes of Hitler after a humiliating defeat in the earlier war:

> There is hardly a parallel in history to Hitler's series of political triumphs in those first years. The reintegration of the Saar . . . a mass arms buildup . . . the occupation of the Rhineland . . . the "annexation" of Austria creating the "Grossdeutsches Reich," and, finally, only a few weeks before the November pogroms, the Munich Agreement, the partition of Czechoslovakia. The Versailles Treaty was now really only a scrap of paper . . . the German Reich had suddenly become the hegemonial power of the old continent.

And, perhaps most seriously, by using a matter-of-fact tone that was meant to convey the notion that these opinions were not at all extraordinary for the time, Jenninger vividly called to mind the suspicion and contempt that many Germans felt toward Jews:

And as for the Jews: hadn't they in the past arrogated a role unto themselves that they did not deserve? Wasn't there a need for them to finally start accepting restrictions? Hadn't they even perhaps merited being put in their place? And, above all, didn't the propaganda – aside from wild exaggerations not to be taken seriously – correspond . . . to people's own suspicions and convictions?

Nevertheless, Jenninger's overriding purpose clearly was to engage in a serious moral discourse. For he dealt directly with the horrors that were to come, seeing in them the unavoidable conclusion of the Nazis' political logic:

After this the death factories were built . . . The offenders replaced the executioner with grotesquely exaggerated industrial methods of vermin control – in keeping with what they said regarding the need to "exterminate vermin." We do not want to close our eyes to this last and very horrible fact. Dostoevski once said: "If God did not exist, everything would be permitted." . . . [This] turned out to be a prophetic anticipation of the political crimes of the twentieth century.[13]

He went on to quote from an SS man's account of the mass killings of many hundreds of machine-gunned Jews; a soldier sits idly, smoking a cigarette, legs dangling over the edge of a huge pit that is being filled with the bodies of Jewish victims. Even on the printed page, the passage is shocking. That, of course, is what Jenninger intended. Yet by speaking in this way he was doubly offensive, paying insufficient deference to the sensibilities of the descendants of both the victims and the perpetrators of the Holocaust. Telling this particular, unpalatable truth in the way in which he did violated an unannounced but commonly understood taboo and cost him his political career.

Philipp Jenninger's experience illustrates a complex social reality. His personal sentiments, as evidenced by a lifetime in politics, could not have caused his downfall. On the contrary, it was his liberal reputation that led him to believe that he could get away with such a graphic "truth-telling."[14] And, although everyone acknowledged the literal truth of his claims, in the end this seemed not to matter. Many even affirmed the importance of his evident goal for the speech – namely to encourage modern Germans to look candidly at their history, the better to avoid repeating it. Still, by violating a taboo against any expression that might be construed as sympathetic to this period in German history, by upsetting an etiquette of discourse that prevents the full truth of the period from being faced, and by failing to limit himself to platitudes that, although showing due deference to collective sensibility, cannot possibly advance the moral discussion, he committed an unforgivable offense.

Jenninger, it could be said, suffered the wrath of political correctness. But glibly comparing this event with the problems of people who depart from some aspects of campus orthodoxy risks missing its true significance. The narrowing of the public discourse in his national community that Jenninger's fate underscores is a profound phenomenon, which reflects powerful social forces at work in many other contexts. Analyzing these forces is far more valuable than taking comfort in denouncing their consequences.

The case at hand illustrates how *the effective examination of fundamental moral questions can be impeded by the superficial moralism of expressive conventions. If exploring an ethical problem requires expressing oneself in ways that raise doubts about one's basic moral commitments, then people may opt for the mouthing of right-sounding but empty words over the risks of substantive moral analysis.* The irony here is exquisite. For, although the desire to police speakers' morality underlies the taboo, the sanitized public expression that results precludes the honest examination of the historical and current circumstances from which genuine moral understanding might arise. As we shall see, discussion of racial issues in the United States is plagued by a similar problem.

Another point worth noting is that Jenninger was apparently unable to create sufficient space between his spoken words (which in some of the most offensive passages were not even his own, but rather those of some long defunct propagandist) and his intended meaning. He failed to bracket or frame his utterances about the realities of the Nazi era in such a way that the listeners might clearly distinguish between a recounting of others' feelings and an expression of one's own. Once he began to talk in a certain way, the words had a life and meaning of their own, uncontrollable through any explicit qualification that he might have – and has since – issued. I elaborate further, in Section 5, on the fact that it is often not possible to exempt oneself from punishment for deviant speech through a simple declaration of innocuous intent.

B   *The Sanctions Debate*

In the mid to late 1980s we all knew that solidarity with the struggle of Blacks in South Africa required the US government to impose trade sanctions against that nation and American universities to divest themselves of stock in companies that were doing business there. Nobel laureate Desmond Tutu and Rev. Allen Boesak, spokesmen for the African National Congress repeatedly said so – and so did Black American anti-apartheid activists. People genuinely committed to justice did not become entangled in arcane technical arguments about the effects of economic boycotts. Nor were they unduly concerned about the possibly deleterious impact of sanctions imposed on Black South Africans, because the most visible proponent of *that* argument was the racist government. Remarkably, even those South Africans who had spent a lifetime fighting apartheid but who opposed sanctions because they thought that the policy would do more harm than good (Helen Suzman, for example) were not taken seriously by American activists.

Because President Reagan's policy of constructive engagement was universally viewed by campus activists as morally bankrupt, few college administrators openly countered demands for divestment with the plausible claim that, instead of selling stocks, the institutions could accomplish more by being constructively engaged, through educational exchanges and the like, with the South African people. Moreover, even to propose an analysis of the impact of sanctions when the judgment as to their advisability was contingent upon the outcome was to tread on politically dangerous ground. There was consensus, among decent people, on the need to stand in solidarity with victims of racism.

Consider the dilemma of a politically liberal university president during this period. Whether or not that person believed in the efficacy of the sanctions policy, he could not credibly claim to be ignorant either of what this action had come to mean in effect or of the students' knowledge of *his* awareness of its meaning. If nevertheless the president chose to resist student demands for radical change in university investment policies, saying that "divestment is a well-intentioned but unwise policy for our university and there are better ways for us to proceed," then he must have intended for the students to draw the inference

that their president was an obstructionist, someone opposed to doing a "progressive" thing.[15]
Most college administrators and trustees who
were suspicious about the morality or wisdom
of divestment found the prospect of this reaction
from students to be unpalatable.

It is plausible to suppose that those college
presidents with a greater than average commitment to the fight against racism would have been
more concerned than the typical administrator
about adverse student reactions. Thus, although
they may have considered divestment unwise,
such people, not wanting to risk damage to their
reputations as good liberals, would have succumbed early to student pressures to divest. Over
time, those college administrators who openly
resisted divestment turned out more and more
to be persons who, through their other public
utterances and actions, had demonstrated a lack
of loyalty to progressive causes. This made it even
more difficult for their genuinely progressive but
suspicious colleagues to voice their doubts about
divestment – or, for that matter, about the tactics
employed by student protesters in promoting the
policy (tents on the campus green and occupation
of administrative offices). In the end, resistance

to the policy became an accurate signal of lack of commitment to the cause, because the truly committed who doubted the virtues of the policy had censored themselves, while the truly uncommitted continued to oppose the policy openly.[16] This process took place not just on campuses, but in legislatures and on op-ed pages as well.[17]

An important consequence of these developments was that a sustained rational discussion of the many complex ethical and political considerations raised by the sanctions policy and by the tactics used to promote it simply did not take place on the campuses in those years. Decisions were taken without the benefits of full analysis and debate. This highlights an elemental and potentially dangerous logic, which can operate in a climate of self-censorship:

> *A certain course of action is imbued with a symbolic meaning in effect, quite apart from the real-world consequences of its pursuit. Expression of doubt about the wisdom of this course of action is suppressed because dissenters want not to be labeled as deviant from some communal norm. As a result, the policy is pursued willy-nilly, and on a broad scale, with perhaps benign but perhaps disastrous consequences. Because the alternatives*

are never properly studied, one cannot be sure. In any
case, the consequences, which should be the primary con-
sideration, become subordinated to the goal of expressing
virtuous sentiments.

I am not arguing that the sanctions policy
was disastrous, merely that it was often pursued
without due consideration for its objective consequences, or sometimes in spite of what was
thought to be the likely results.[18] Perhaps as
importantly to the universities, decisions about
the handling of students' protests in support of
the policy were colored by a concern for the negative impression that applying discipline in that
context was sure to attract. The inaction of those
years set precedents that have outlived the sanctions "debate."

Moreover, instead of a university's decision
on divestment, consider a nation's decision on
whether to wage war or a union's decision on
whether to strike. The same dangerous logic
may well apply. Yet now, when opposition to
the proposed course of action takes on a meaning in effect that precludes vigorous deliberation
over the merits of that course, the result may be
that enormously harmful actions – the kinds of

actions that affect millions of lives – would be wrongly undertaken.[19]

C   A Classic Political Witch Hunt

As a final illustration, consider the climate of opinion that must have prevailed in a congressional hearing room in the 1940s and 1950s, when investigations into the loyalty of prominent Americans were openly conducted. It was commonly understood at the time that the United States faced a formidable adversary in a cold war and that many US citizens sympathized with the ideals espoused by this adversary. It was considered entirely appropriate that steps be taken to protect the national interest against possibly disloyal acts committed by these misguided souls. Some of these steps, to be sure, raised constitutional questions, but one had to weigh this against the relative importance of liberty and security. After all, there were real communists among us, committed to advancing the agenda of the Soviet Union. Besides, who exactly were these people, who voiced such vehement procedural objections to the deployment of reasonable safeguards against possibly damaging breaches of security? Just what kind of person would, under the circumstances, quibble about the civil liberties of a few communists and their fellow travelers?

The Soviet Union was expanding rapaciously into Eastern Europe; the Red Guards had taken over in Beijing; the State Department had apparently been infiltrated; atomic secrets had been stolen. Under these circumstances, what kind of people quibbled over such details as whether some line of questioning comports entirely with the existing standards of due process? Could we not infer something about their values from their refusal to name names, or from their willingness to speak openly on behalf of an accused? Perhaps those objecting to our methods of inquiry should themselves be sanctioned.[20]

In such a climate, an anti-communist civil libertarian who wants not to be mistaken for a fellow traveler may find silence to be the wisest course. And those bent on ferreting out the deviants would probably find that they can say just about anything about just about anyone, without being called to account for it. The more widespread the silence among unquestionably loyal Americans and the more prominent the fellow travelers among those who protest against the witch hunt, the more reliably does protesting send a signal of political belief. A demagogue like Wisconsin Senator Joseph McCarthy could enjoy a prolonged career under such circumstances. When people, once they became targets, can be smeared with lies and innuendo ("I have in my hand a list of names"), and when guilt can be based on a decades-old association with a suspicious cause, caution must be the rule of the day. Such caution plays right into the hands of the demagogues.

A generic problem with the conventions of value signaling is the ease with which they can be abused by partisan opportunists. When listeners are keen to discern a speaker's basic values on a crucial issue, that speaker has to worry that his political enemies will, by distorting or misrepresenting his expressions, falsely depict him as being morally unsound. He has to take care, in other words, not to be *smeared*. To minimize this risk, the speaker may need to avoid some issues altogether, or to speak only in the most circumspect and indirect way, especially if he is criticizing the consensus view. Pointed remarks on a sensitive topic lend themselves to caricature and distortion.

Thus, and again ironically, the public's heightened moral sensitivity, together with a political climate of intense partisan conflict, may actually result in a lower level of effective moral discourse, as the making of nuanced arguments and the drawing of fine distinctions become too risky for political speakers.

The smear campaign as an instrument of political warfare was made famous during the McCarthy period. This had a clear and lasting effect on the formulation of foreign policy. Arguments about relations with communist China, for example, were encumbered with a host of collateral meanings, thereby inhibiting public discourse.[21] Moreover, unprincipled conservatives tried to pin the "commie" label on political enemies whose real offense was to hold liberal views on domestic policy.[22] More recently, the public's desire to infer a political figure's true values on race and gender issues has been exploited in this way for partisan purposes. The nominees of Reagan and Bush, lacking the benefits of a track record that gave them credible "cover" against the charge of being racists, have been especially vulnerable to this sort of smear tactic.[23]

5 Implications for the Character and Effectiveness of Public Debate

A   The Futility of Protesting Too Much

All of these examples illustrate an important feature of regimes of tacit censorship: one cannot break their grip through a simple declaration of sincerity. ("Despite my violation of the norm, please understand that my values are pure.") Reliance on such literal claims is a common mode of naive behavior in the forum. The act of making the claim may itself become a signal of the claimant's deviance. When a form of expression has the meaning in effect that those who speak in this way are likely to have "bad" values, a speaker's overt demands for credibility or complaints about the limits placed on his freedom of expression quickly become futile. *Conventions of tacit restraint in public expression are made more durable by the fact that they do not themselves easily become objects of criticism, because it is often the truly deviant who have the greatest interest in criticizing them.*

Meta-argumentation – arguing at the secondary level about the form that primary arguments should be allowed to take in the community – can become the refuge of scoundrels who seek to avoid the righteous condemnation that their morally dubious expressions have earned. And it is indeed the case that complaints about the "reign of terror" of political correctness on campuses, even when not exaggerated, have had little effect on the administrators, professors, or student activists enthusiastic about one or the other of the favored "correct" causes. Complaints about political correctness, though divorced from any explicit advocacy for a policy position, nevertheless have the faint but distinct odor of conservatism about them.

We all know the formula "Some of my best friends are . . . but . . .," as in "Some of my best friends are Blacks, but their affirmative action claims have gone too far," or "Some of my best friends are Jews, but Israel's policies are barbaric," and the like. Note that this verbal construction is no longer used literally; instead it now serves as a sarcastic reference to people who unsuccessfully affect a concern for values they do not really share. The strange career of this locution – its literal meaning having been overtaken by a symbolic one – highlights the fact that strategic political expression has become much more salient in American public life.

Literal use of this type of sentence is now patently naive. Although its purpose is to spare the speaker ill judgment or criticism of his values as the "but" clause is uttered, it serves instead to alert listeners that a bigot's statement is about to come. Listeners know that the speaker is aware that people who make such statements are suspected of racism (or anti-Semitism, misogyny, sympathy for communism, homophobia, etc.); after all, issuing the qualification acknowledges the suspicious nature of such talk. What type of person, the listener then asks, requests this exemption?

Those, for example, who genuinely value racial equality know that, even if they harbor reservations about affirmative action, in the interest of supporting a good and decent policy they ought not to utter them. And those less interested in racial equality can be relied upon to see no such constraint. So not only will "progressives" abstain from criticizing affirmative action, they will also not complain about not being able to express their criticisms!

About the person who argues for the right to tell a racial joke by prefacing his argument with "Some of my best friends are Blacks, but. . ." we must say, "methinks he doth protest too much."

Under a convention of restrained public expression, prudent people do not protest for the right to say imprudent things.

B   Strategic Imprecision

In "Politics and the English Language," George Orwell, describing the poor state into which political writing had fallen in postwar England, observed:

> The word *Fascism* has now no meaning except in so far as it signifies "something not desirable" . . . a word like *democracy* not only [has] . . . no agreed definition, but the attempt to make one is resisted from all sides. It is almost universally felt that when we call a country democratic we are praising it: consequently the defenders of every kind of regime claim that it is a democracy, and fear that they might have to stop using the word if it were tied down to any one meaning. Words of this kind are often used in a consciously dishonest way . . . the person who uses them has his own private definition, but allows his hearer to think he means something quite different.[24]

This is an insightful observation, directly relevant to the present discussion. It is clear that ambiguous and imprecise talk is a valuable tactic for the strategic speaker. By expressing himself in generalities, a sender allows various receivers to impute their own, possibly inconsistent, meanings to his pronouncements. With a euphemism well chosen for its vagueness, a speaker can say palatably (that is, in a manner that coheres with existent communal norms) what, if said more incisively, might offend some listeners. The circumlocution may be intended to deceive or merely to obscure, but in either case the result is a debasement of the currency of public discourse.

Consider, for example, some uses of the term "minorities" in contemporary American public speech. The speaker may actually mean "Blacks," but find that term embarrassingly specific. (This is usually the case when the reference is to some aspect of urban life that has negative connotations.) Or, as with the phrase "women and minorities," the speaker may hope, through the use of words alone, to create a coalition of interests in the listener's mind, when none exists in fact. Or, finally, consider a recent addition to the progressive lexicon: "disadvantaged minorities." One finds this phrase used in educational and philanthropic circles when the speaker really means "non-Whites, excluding Asians." Never mind the fact that many Asians are disadvantaged! Imagine the uproar, were a foundation to announce, candidly, a scholarship program intended to help "non-White persons belonging to groups that perform poorly on standardized tests." So the strategic speaker sacrifices honesty and accuracy by declaring instead that the program is aimed at "disadvantaged minorities." A variation on this theme is the "underrepresented minority" – though in current times talk of any minority group as being "over-represented" is clearly taboo.[25]

Such linguistic imprecision impairs analysis. But this is often its purpose. The person who utters the phrase "women and minorities" may want not to reckon with the fact that the majority of women, being married to White men, share significant resources and fundamental interests with their putative oppressors. An advocate for "diversity" may prefer not to be explicit about which differences are included and which are excluded from that advocacy (religious and political beliefs, for example). No sane person could relish the task of explaining to poor but studious Vietnamese immigrants why they do not qualify for some "minority" scholarships. And if one wants to accommodate more "underrepresented" Black and Hispanic students at a university by admitting fewer Whites, but not fewer Asians, then one surely would rather not dwell on the statistical "overrepresentation" of the latter.

Another way in which the lack of clear language can be helpful is illustrated by *the use of emblematic speech to signal moral values.* The speaker advertises his beliefs by using words in a way that, for political or aesthetic reasons, someone who does not hold those beliefs would never emulate. Then the speech act has the effect of waving a banner: "queers," "at-risk group," "institutional racism," "fascist America," "differently abled person." When words are spoken in a given manner only by those who hold a discrete set of opinions, their use in this way signals that the speakers adhere to their party's position.

Two strangers conversing on an airplane feel each other out to learn whether they have similar views on matters it would be better to avoid, were they to become a source of disagreement. Such conversations involve the tentative and halting display of one's position through the use of emblematic speech. Each speaker, seeking recognition and reinforcement, looks for the positive feedback that encourages that candor in discussion possible only among the like-minded. The dialogue may grow into an intense and intimate exchange or may lapse into vague and meaningless banter, depending on what the speakers are able to learn about each other. If real communication eventually occurs, the path to it will have been paved by overtures of calculated imprecision.

Alternatively, consider a political speaker addressing a crowd in the forum. If the significance of some words as signals of belief is known only to insiders, their use in public allows the speaker to convey a reassuring message to some listeners – "I share your values" – without alarming the others. These words are *coded emblems of belief*. A racist politician might use code words – "welfare queen," "criminal element," "states' rights" – to appeal to like-minded voters, while maintaining what in the intelligence world is called "plausible deniability" when it comes to his motive: if challenged, the speaker exploits the code words' ambiguity of meaning and claims that he intended no offense. Once words become emblems in this way, speakers with different values who want not to risk being misunderstood must abandon using them altogether.

C   Multiple Audiences

The use of code words is characteristic of a situation in which the speaker faces multiple audiences – distinct communities of listeners that do not share communal norms. This situation is rich with strategic possibilities. The presence of distinct audiences may induce more candid expressions, as each group keeps the speaker honest on issues of concern to the other.[26] Or, if one audience is naive and the other sophisticated, a duplicitous speaker may talk over the heads of the naive listeners to get his true message across to those in the know.[27] Another possibility, frequently observed with discussion in mixed company, is that *standing to address an issue is restricted to a certain class of persons, who have what I will call "natural cover."* These are people who, because of their group identity, are not immediately presumed to have malign motives for expressing themselves in a potentially offensive way.

Thus Blacks, but not Whites, can make movies or report news stories on the problem of skin color prejudice, which continues to affect African American society. Women, but not men, can publicly question whether in a given case the crime of date rape has been manufactured on the morning

49

after by a "victim" who wishes she had made a different decision about sexual intimacy the previous night. Censorship in these cases is partial; those who have cover express themselves freely; those who lack it must be silent. When the combination of an ascriptive trait with an offending expression is necessary to mark the speaker as "bad," words spoken in mixed company have a meaning in effect that is contingent upon the matter of who has spoken them. A White is taken to be a racist if he says "nigger," but Blacks use the word all the time. Used by Blacks, its value ranges from term of endearment to epithet; but, for Whites, whatever their intent, it can only be an epithet.

When the effective meaning of some expression is contingent on both the speaker and the audience, the rules of permissible expression in mixed company will generally differ from those applicable to homogeneous gatherings. Men talking among themselves have rules concerning what can decently be said about women, but these rules are generally less restrictive than the ones governing a mixed conversation. This is one reason why the "token woman" – the only woman present at a table of men – can be more than marginally significant. She may have only one vote but, by her presence, even without saying a word, she can profoundly influence the tone and substance of the debate by narrowing the boundaries of legitimate discourse.[28]

Notice also that, when the rules of permissible expression vary with the audience, prudent speakers must be sure to remember whom they are addressing at any moment. And they must also worry about how an expression formulated in one context will "sound" in another. Indeed, a common source of the political gaffe is news media's rendering in public of a remark made privately, in a setting where different rules applied. For example, Jesse Jackson's gaffe during the 1984 presidential campaign, when he referred to New York City as "Hymietown," was made in front of an all Black audience of reporters and staff. Although he should not have spoken like that even there, his intention was probably less malign than the anti-Semitic meaning ascribed to his remark after the matter became public. Still, once the remark was out in the open, the *ad hominem* query – "What kind of person speaks, even privately, in this way?" – became irresistible.[29]

An interesting feature of multiple audience situations is that *sometimes it is insiders, not out-*

siders, who are specifically forbidden to voice certain opinions or address certain issues in mixed company. "Washing dirty linen in public" refers to injudicious speech by an insider that is taboo in mixed company, but that would be appropriate if no outsiders were present. This can be speech – especially criticism of one's group – in which outsiders routinely engage. The taboo may derive from a concern that outsiders would misinterpret the information, a fear that the insider's words would be exploited by outsiders against the group's interest, or a worry that outsiders will feel legitimized in their own criticism of the group, once an insider has confirmed it.

In general, conflict or competition between groups in an audience changes the strategic implications of critical expression. If a partisan opponent criticizes our party, we respond by saying that the critic doesn't know what he's talking about, and in any case seeks only to discredit us. If one of our own makes the same criticism, no such defense is available; moreover, our opponents are emboldened to make some points of their own. The insider critic is more persuasive than the outsider because he has superior information about group functioning and his criticism is more likely to be motivated by a genuine concern for the group's welfare. For these reasons groups often try to discourage insider criticism by punishing the members who engage in it – a tendency that has important implications for the ethics and efficacy of public discourse.[30]

I am often struck by the intensity of critical debate among Black Americans over such issues as the social problems of the "underclass" when that debate takes place out of the hearing of Whites. The same theme, when explored by a Black speaker in mixed company, causes other Blacks to severely sanction him as a deviant. Similarly, if a White gives voice in mixed company to his fear of criminal victimization, he may be perceived as criticizing Blacks. (And that could indeed be his intent.) This perception will be enough to keep some Whites, but not all, from expressing their fear. But if a Black in that audience supports or confirms the White's feeling when everyone knows that a complaint over the "criminal element" has racial connotations, he courts serious trouble with other Blacks. So does the Black who worries publicly about the fairness of affirmative action.

In these three examples, the Blacks are expressing themselves in ways that cause their fellows to question their basic commitments. They are seen as violating a cardinal principle of group loyalty by departing from the convention of restrained expression – although, as Albert Hirschman (1970) has noted, the willingness to deviate in the face of a sanction for the sake of the group's welfare, as one understands it, might be seen as an expression of true loyalty. It is therefore not surprising that *these deviants are often accused of being racially inauthentic*. In the minds of blind loyalists, breaking the "no group criticism in mixed company" taboo raises the question of whether the critics are genuinely Black.[31]

And yet, as Michael Walzer has observed, in a democracy serious political analysis cannot take place in private, among Blacks alone, out of Whites' hearing. So, by making racial authenticity contingent on rhetorical conformity, the blind loyalists succeed in diminishing the vitality of the American political forum.

6 Forbidden Facts

The French intellectual Jean-François Revel (1983), lamenting the difficulty of keeping the truth about the Soviet Union before the Western European public, observed: "It is around the circulation of facts that the taboos are strongest in the evolution of public information and debate into national policy. . . . As a rule, concern that a fact might influence public opinion in a way we dislike overrides our curiosity about it and our honesty in making it known" (pp. 24–5). Revel identified three reasons for these taboos. (1) Leftists who embraced socialist ideals saw criticism of the Soviet Union as a disguised attack on socialism; thus they avoided it themselves and looked askance at people willing to sound the alarm. (2) Conservatives seeking a more militaristic posture justified their policy arguments by characterizing the Soviets as aggressors. So, to counter their arguments, evidence of Soviet aggression had to be denied. (3) The prospect that the nuclear superpower in the East might actually pose a threat to European democracies was so frightening that many people simply preferred to deny the reality of the threat, hiding their heads in the sand.

These observations are relevant to our general analysis of censored public discussion. Notice that points (1) and (2) both involve strategic factors: if reporting a fact symbolizes that the reporter has "bad" values, or if it strengthens the hand of those on the "wrong" side in a public debate, then prudent people with "good" values, who want to be seen as standing on the "right" side of history, do not report that fact. If some truth about the world is inconsistent with a firmly held communal value, listeners may punish the messenger who asserts that truth, reasoning that only someone who disdains the value in question would act so as to undermine it. Anticipating this punishment, investigators will be dissuaded not only from saying what they know but also from asking questions that could have unpleasant answers. When rhetoric about facts comes in this way to signal one's values on an important ethical matter, the identification and analysis of significant social problems can be impeded.

This problem is classically illustrated in the historic conflicts between religion and science. Galileo was forced by the church to recant his views; Christian fundamentalists have attacked the teaching of evolution theory. But in our time other, secular motivations for suppressing facts and limiting the analysis loom even larger. Scientists looking into the genetic basis, if any, of gender or racial differences in behavior have met with vocal opposition from "women and minorities" who regard the very act of speculating about this to be evidence of bigotry. The search for biological factors that influence violent behavior has been denounced as racist, although this plausible hypothesis has no evidently racial connotation. Yet, ironically, the view that sexual preference *is not* rooted in biology has been denounced as well, and by the very same people!

In line with my theory that expression is often curtailed for fear of offending communal norms, one finds that the pressure on researchers not to carry out an investigation, or to withhold its findings, often originates *within* scientific communities, not without.[32] This is especially so in the social sciences. Sociologist James Coleman, perhaps the world's leading scholar of educational policy, recalls that in 1976 the president and a number of prominent members of the American Sociological Association (ASA) tried to have him censured for the "crime" of discovering, and announcing, that citywide busing for school desegregation purposes caused White flight (i.e. the large-scale migration of White people). This claim had been denied for years before Coleman's research, and far-reaching social policies were erected on the presumption that it was not true. We now know that Coleman was right. The taboos that prevented the circulation of facts and that were then prevalent among American sociologists had seriously deleterious consequences. Yet, when Coleman presented his work at the ASA meetings that year, the corridors outside the lecture hall and the wall behind the podium from which he had to speak were covered with posters displaying, along with his name and the title of his talk, Nazi swastikas and other epithets to the effect that he was a racist.[33]

Some areas of social science inquiry are so closely linked in the public mind to sensitive issues of policy that an objective scholarly discussion of them is now impossible. Instead of open debate – where participants are prepared to be persuaded by arguments and evidence contrary to their initial presumptions – we have become accustomed to rhetorical contests – where competing camps fire volleys of data and tendentious analyses at each other, back and forth, in an effort to win public opinion to their side. Sometimes the press is an active participant in these struggles, selectively reporting the findings that confirm the politically correct point of view. Issues of race, gender, and sexual preference are particularly susceptible to this process of politicization.

Investigators identifying with certain groups advocate approaches to their disciplines that allegedly reflect their particular perspective – a feminist, a Black, or a gay approach to history, sociology, economics, anthropology, and so on. This fragmentation, now well advanced and seemingly irreversible, whatever one may think of it, is closely connected to the fact that *public rhetoric in many areas of the social sciences is self-consciously undertaken as a multiple audience talk.* The disciplines are not insular venues of discourse, governed by internal norms of scholarly expression accepted by all who have been trained to do research in the field. Social scientists not only address each other; they participate in a larger discussion, which has extra-scientific implications. Perhaps it was always like this, although growth of the regulatory and welfare state has undoubtedly enlarged the extent to which scientific expression has political consequences.

The notion of objective research – say, on the effects of the minimum wage on employment, or on the influence of maternal employment on child development – can have no meaning if, when the results are reported, other "scientists" are mainly concerned with raising the *ad hominem* query: "Just what kind of economist, sociologist, and so on would say this?" Not only will investigators be induced to censor themselves, the very way in which research is evaluated and consensus about "the facts" formed will be altered. If, when a study yields unpopular conclusions, it is subjected to greater scrutiny than usual and more effort is expended on its refutation, an obvious bias toward finding what the community is looking for will have been introduced. Thus the very way in which knowledge of the world around us is constituted can be influenced by the phenomenon of strategic expression.

7 Conclusion

There are many questions that remain to be investigated. Why do certain issues seem to be especially effective vehicles for the tacit communication of the values of those who speak and write about them? Who, if anyone, chooses the vocabulary of symbolic expression? When is political correctness – understood as consensual restraint on public expression in a community

– on balance, beneficial? (I have mainly discussed its problematic nature.) What can be done to reverse a regime of rhetorical reticence, once established? What are the responsibilities of individuals within a community whose public discourse on important matters lacks in candor? Is there a role for courage and heroism?

These are matters of great seriousness, raising ethical as well as political questions. Who, we must ask, will speak for compromise and moderation in negotiations, when to speak in this way is seen to signal a weak commitment to "the struggle"? Who will declare the emperor to be naked, when a leader's personal failings hurt the movement? Who will urge, under pressures of economic or electoral competition, that the old ways of doing business in our company or our party require reexamination? Who will report the lynchers, known to everyone in town despite their hooded costumes? Who will expose the terrorists, or denounce the haters, once lynching, terror, and hatred have become "legitimate" means of political expression? Who will insist that we speak plainly and tell the truth about delicate and difficult matters that we would all prefer to cover up or ignore? How can a community sustain an elevated and liberal political discourse, when the social forces that promote tacit censorship threaten to usher in a dark age?

One of the finest statements ever written on these questions, I believe, is Vaclav Havel's essay "The Power of the Powerless" (published in English in Keane 1985). Confronting the overarching repression of the "post-totalitarian system," Havel describes the existential and ideological features of late communism that gave the dissidents their power. "Between the aims of the post-totalitarian system and the aims of life there is a yawning abyss," he writes (p. 29). While life moves toward the "fulfillment of its own freedom," the system demands "conformity, uniformity and discipline." The system is permeated by lies: workers are enslaved in the name of the working class, the expansion of empire is depicted as support for the oppressed, denial of free expression is supposed to be the highest form of freedom, rigged elections are the highest form of democracy, and so on. For the system to continue, individual citizens must make their peace with these lies; they must choose to "live within a lie." The dissident, who quixotically refuses to go along with the program, defiantly attempting to "live within the truth," is profoundly subversive: "By breaking the rules of the game, he has disrupted the game as such. He has exposed it as a mere game. . . . He has said that the emperor is naked. And because the emperor is in fact naked, something extremely dangerous has happened" (pp. 39–40).

Thus the struggle between the "aims of the system" and the "aims of life" takes place not between social classes, or political parties, or aggregates of people aligned on opposite lines, for and against the system. Rather this struggle is fought within each human being (p. 38):

The essential aims of life are present naturally in every person. In everyone there is some longing for humanity's rightful dignity, for moral integrity, for free expression of being and a sense of transcendence over the world of existences. Yet, at the same time, each person is capable, to a greater or lesser degree, of coming to terms with living within the lie. Each person somehow succumbs to a profane trivialization of his or her inherent humanity, and to utilitarianism. In everyone there is some willingness to merge with the anonymous crowd and to flow comfortably along with it down the river of pseudo-life. This is much more than a simple conflict between two identities. It is something far worse: it is a challenge to the very notion of identity itself.

Truth, Havel concludes, has its own special power in the post-totalitarian system: "Under the orderly surface of the life of lies, therefore, there slumbers the hidden sphere of life in its real aims, of its hidden openness to truth" (p. 41).

Although I certainly do not intend to compare the constrained expressive environment of a politically correct college campus with the systematic extirpation of dissent characteristic of the totalitarian state, I nevertheless find the moral dimensions of Havel's argument relevant to the dilemmas faced by individuals in our own society. Conventions of self-censorship are sustained by the utilitarian acquiescence of each community member in an order that, at some level, denies the whole truth: by calculating that the losses derived from deviation outweigh the gains, individuals are led to conform. Yet by doing so they yield something of their individuality and their dignity to "the system." Usually this is a minor matter – more like the small sacrifices we make for the sake of social etiquette – rather than some grand political compromise. But, as I hope to have made clear in the foregoing exposition, circumstances arise when far weightier concerns are at stake. The same calculus is at work in every case.

How, then, are the demagogues and the haters to be denounced? How can reason gain a voice in the forum? How can the truth about our nation, our party, our race, our church come to light, when the social forces of conformity and the rhetorical conventions of banality hold sway? How can we have a genuine moral discourse about ambiguous and difficult matters – such as racial inequality in our cities or on our campuses – when the security and comfort of the platitudes lie so readily at hand? Although it may violate the communal norms of my economics fraternity to say so, I believe that these things can be achieved only when individuals, first a few and then many, transcend "the world of existences" by acting not as utilitarian calculators, but rather as fully human and fully moral agents, determined at whatever cost to "live within the truth."

Acknowledgment

I wish to thank Thomas Schelling, without whose encouragement this article would never have been written. The comments of Timur Kuran, Linda Datcher Loury, and Charles Griswold have also been helpful. I benefited from the opportunity to discuss these ideas in a number of forums, and especially at the Philosophy Department Colloquium at Boston University.

Afterword

Self-Censorship in a Time of War

Early in 2024, I was invited to speak about Black–Jewish relations at a synagogue in Palm Beach, Florida. It was a subject I had spoken and written about before. Still, as the date approached, I grew more and more nervous. What was expected of me? Had I asked the event's organizers, I'm sure they would have said that nothing was expected except that I come and give my view on whatever aspect of the topic interested me, answer some questions from the audience, and attend the lovely meals and receptions they had planned.

But the war was on my mind. The reports of the dead, the grotesque images, and the terrifying accounts of the refugees weighed heavily on me. In the months since Hamas's brutal attack on Israel on October 7, 2023, the death toll in Gaza had been mounting at a dizzying pace. The United States had, in short order, affirmed its support for Israel and was supplying a steady flow of weapons and money, paying only lip service to what I was beginning to view, what I could not help but view, as a humanitarian disaster – not because of the dead Hamas militants and their political leadership, who all knew what they had been signing up for, but because of the dead women, children, and elderly people, because of the dead medics and journalists. The news of dire food shortages in Gaza chilled me, as did images of block after block of bombed out ruins that once housed apartments, schools, and businesses.

Israel had a right to respond to Hamas's attack. Indeed, considering the brutality of the October 7 assault, Israel had a duty and a responsibility to respond. Nevertheless, the killing of thousands upon thousands of noncombatants, while hundreds of thousands were subjected to injury and starvation and the homes of millions were destroyed, seemed to me an unacceptably high cost to pay for the goal of "eliminating" or "eradicating" Hamas, especially since it was unclear whether and how that goal would ever be accomplished. It also seemed likely that the scope of the death and destruction that were wrought would inspire more people in the region and abroad to take up arms against Israel than would have been the case, had its response been less devastating to the civilian population. What was being done in Gaza, if arguably necessary from Israel's point of view, nevertheless amounted to a set of horrific deeds with which I was loath to see my own country associated.

These thoughts troubled me. They made me question my longstanding affirmation of Israel's prerogative to do what it deemed necessary to defend itself, and of my country's support for the same. When I hinted publicly at my growing doubts about Israel's actions in Gaza, I received immediate blowback. Friends and strangers alike were emailing me long missives, taking me to task for my historical ignorance, listing figures about "acceptable" civilian-to-combatant death ratios, and reiterating Israel's embattled regional position. The common refrain that emerged among ardently pro-Israel politicians, media figures, spokesmen, and others was this: to suggest that Israel was killing too many civilians amounted to a betrayal of the Jewish people. I chafed at this idea. I knew I was not – am not – an anti-Semite, but it soon became clear to me that giving voice to my misgivings about Israel's conduct of this war risked having me labeled as one.

The date of the speech loomed. I would never conflate the Jewish people and the State of Israel. But, from what I knew of that synagogue and the organizers, I would be speaking to people who, more likely than not, would object to any criticism of Israel's conduct in the war. I felt that to march into a synagogue that had gone out of its way to welcome me and then, without warning, to say things I knew would be grievously offensive to the sensibilities of those assembled would have been extraordinarily rude.

Still, this was an urgent matter. For Gazans and Israelis, yes, but also, in a different way, for us Americans. The US logistical and diplomatic support for the war was a point of heated conflict on college campuses such as Brown's, where I teach. The pro-Palestinian side did have its excesses, and some true anti-Semites were taking advantage of it, but that did not negate, for me, the moral and prudential core of the arguments for a ceasefire coupled with the release of Israeli hostages.

I chose not to raise the subject of the war at all at that synagogue. But I didn't avoid the topic out of mere politeness. Up to that point, on my podcast, *The Glenn Show*, I had merely dropped hints that I was uncomfortable with America's role in the war. But I was afraid of what taking an explicit, full-throated position critical of Israel's military response would do to my reputation. I was wary that the issue was so charged that I could lose friends over it. And I knew that some readers and viewers of my comments would infer the worst: that I was taking sides against the Jewish state, and hence against the Jewish people. These perceived pressures – and some of them are more than merely "perceived" – have led me to approach the topic tentatively, and sometimes even to hold my tongue, whereas I normally have no problem speaking my mind, even when I know that my views are unpopular.

And so I found myself in this position of self-censorship at the synagogue. I opted to avoid the topic entirely rather than risk coming out as a true critic of the war. Paradoxically, I was very much aware of the social and psychological processes at work as I elected not to speak about what I believed to be the most pressing of subjects. (It is a tribute to the power of self-censorship that it can take hold even when one knows how it works and why it ought to be resisted.) In "Self-Censorship in Public Discourse" I explain how a process of directing one's inferences against the person – what I call *ad hominem* inference – blocks the open exchange of views on divisive issues. It is a process whereby listeners judge speakers not only on the basis of what is said but also on the basis of what may reasonably be concluded about their unstated values and ulterior motives. Knowing this to happen, speakers choose their words carefully. Silence is often the best option.

If this was true of the political correctness debate when I published that essay, more than three decades ago, it is true in spades of the debate about Israel and Palestine today. Whatever I may say about Gaza – whether I say that I believe the Israel Defense Forces' actions to be heinous crimes, fully justifiable defensive measures, or something in between – this will spur my audience to infer information not explicitly stated about my ostensibly concealed personal beliefs and about my character. The key question for many will become: "Just what kind of person says something like that?" Thus, if I say, "Israel must go to whatever lengths it deems necessary to defend itself," some will infer that I hate Palestinians or care little for their safety. By contrast, if I say, "Israel must bear some moral responsibility for the high number of dead noncombatants," some will infer that I hate the Jewish people or care little for its safety. I can protest that the inference is untrue, but in either case such denials would do little to exonerate me in the eyes of those who take such statements to be nothing but the acceptable public face of nefarious private beliefs. This is particularly so if others, known to have nefarious beliefs, are making similar statements.

Here's another adverse inference: that I am a dupe or a pawn who doesn't know his own mind and I've been hoodwinked by the public relations campaign set up by one side or the other in this conflict. And here are yet others: that I seek to curry favor with supporters of the side I'm defending; or that my private beliefs are misaligned with what I say publicly. If my speech happens to align perfectly with your own, you'll be inclined to think, "He's one of us." You'll be more likely to infer that, whatever my private beliefs are, they are similar to your own.

This private beliefs-signaling game could go on forever. The list of adverse inferences about someone who publicly addresses a controversial subject in an unpopular manner is as long as the list of possible audiences. Again, there is no such thing as a context-free speech. Standing before a congregation at a synagogue is one context; dining at the home of a close friend whom I know to hold staunchly pro-Zionist views is another; writing the Afterword to a book addressed to a general readership is yet another. Moreover, given the realities of digital communication, we must allow that something said in one context will be available in all the others. Tailoring one's message so that it will be understood by every possible audience in the way the speaker intends would be so complex as to be practically impossible. Hence mistaken *ad hominem* inferences are virtually guaranteed.

I spin out a bit of my theory not to distract from the issue at hand, but to explain what I think the issue *really is*. For in some sense my views about Gaza, like those of most individuals, are of little consequence. I'm not a politician, a Middle East expert, a military strategist, or a professor of international relations. I'm commenting as a reasonably well-informed social critic rather than as a specialist. No one with any power to affect the situation on the ground in Gaza would ever hire me as an advisor, nor should they. Even so, what I have said publicly about the war has been closely attended to. This is understandable. The stakes are enormously high for those directly enmeshed in the conflict. They seek allies wherever they can find them. As a result, the *ad hominem* inferential heat has been turned up for those of us lucky enough to be able to comment from the sidelines rather than to experience the front lines. Anyone talking about Gaza, whatever the nuances of their argument, is sorted into the "friend" pile or the "enemy" pile and is treated accordingly. There is no third pile.

This is our ever present condition when speaking about any controversial issue in public. But there is a difference between being branded, say, an "enemy of high corporate taxes" and an "enemy of the Jewish people." Plenty of respectable folks have no problem wearing the former label, but no respectable folks should want to wear the latter. In fact, wanting to wear that label ought *ipso facto* to exclude one from the realm of respectability. We can debate how to tax corporations, but there should be no debate at all about the humanity of the Jews. This is why adverse *ad hominem* inferences about the critics of Israel's conduct in this war – the conclusion that the critic harbors Jew-hatred – can be so damaging.

This is my point, then. I am not an enemy of Israel, but I have problems with what its military is currently doing and with its influence on American foreign policy. I am certainly not an enemy of the Jewish people – I could run down my *bona fides* on that account, but what would I say? "Some of my best friends are Jewish"? (It's true, though.) I loathe the anti-Semites who use protest against Israel to gin up hatred for Jews, but I admire those sincere protestors and activists who want to put a stop to the unnecessary bloodshed and an end to the humanitarian crisis.

Having just read the preceding paragraph, some of you, if you were not already decided, have sorted me into one pile or the other. This leaves me to perform a calculation of my own: at what point does the cost of speaking my mind outweigh the benefit? At that Palm Beach synagogue, I performed that calculation and determined that the personal costs of speaking my mind outweighed the benefits. I kept my mouth shut about Gaza. I have felt shame about that silence ever since.

It can be argued that we should all be willing to risk the consequences of free expression, if we truly believe in the causes and ideas that move us. But how many can afford to lose their livelihoods over a principle? As for me, I am in my eighth decade of life now, at the end of an illustrious academic career. I could, if I so choose, never work another day and still live out the rest of my life in comfort. Perhaps, then, the personal stakes are not as high as I have made them out to be.

But this is not only about me. It's about us. And the stakes are high enough. The repressive aspects of self-censorship make themselves known most spectacularly when they fail, when someone says the "quiet" part out loud, pronounces an unthinkable thought, or otherwise refuses to countenance the social pressure to conform to expectations.

When self-censorship fails, it does so overtly. When it works, it works tacitly. When a prominent figure is "canceled" for uttering a thought deemed noxious by some audience or another, his public punishment serves an unspoken warning to all who may agree with him: shut up, or this will happen to you. Conversely, should a "naked emperor" be finally exposed and should the prior conspiracy of silence about his scandalous condition come undone, this is bound to happen in full view of us all.

The risk of self-censorship, then, is not so much that our public intellectuals and political leaders will be repressed, but that private citizens will be. If we cannot know what our friends, family, neighbors, and community truly think because they fear reprisal, we cannot know ourselves. Social life abhors a discursive vacuum, and where self-censorship imposes diffident silence, true evil can creep in. We need only look to the former Soviet satellite nations to see how silence, enforced by fear, will be filled with suspicion, betrayal, and the shattering of social bonds.

We can calculate the cost of speaking out. But how can we possibly calculate the cost of shutting up? We can enumerate the catastrophes that have resulted when ordinary people in a position to stop a great wrong instead did nothing, believing that they could not bear the cost of speaking out because they could not be sure they had the support of their fellows. It could be argued that those who remained silent did not know the price of that silence until it was already too late. One wonders what tragedies could have been averted, how much suffering avoided, had everyone known the others' minds.

There is a reason why certain opinions are often met with censorious opposition: that is an efficient way to control the discourse. You can't silence everyone – but then you don't have to. Destroy the reputations of a few prominent people, and everyone who agrees with them will fall into line. Level the *ad hominem* attack – "He thinks that because he's anti-Semitic" – and the substantive issues get drowned out, while an unpopular speaker struggles to defend, not his ideas or thoughts, but his very person. A pall of suspicion falls over him. He's sorted into one pile or the other.

Once that sorting has taken place, no amount of self-exculpatory pleading can undo it. When a person's character is assassinated, it tends to stay dead, and not even the corrective of historical hindsight can revive it. Silence, as a self-defensive measure, has its appeal. But those of us who defend free speech have a special responsibility to speak our minds openly when we feel – when we *know* – that the others who share our views will not or cannot do the same. We're inevitably placed in a vulnerable position, for even audiences that would in principle affirm the necessity of speaking out sometimes attempt to squelch the speech they disdain.

It hurts to lose an ally, a friend, or an audience because they no longer consider you on their side. But that personal pain is part of the cost we must be willing to pay, if the alternative is to remain silent even as we know that it is our responsibility to speak up. Holding one's tongue rather than heedlessly airing one's thoughts can be an act of mercy. Distinguishing between politeness, mercy, and a stifling self-censorship requires inner vigilance and insight into one's own motives. Those skills can be kept sharp only through practice. So, whatever its social origins, the fundamental activity of self-censorship takes place within each of us, as individuals. It may well turn out that I couldn't afford the social cost of speaking my mind on Gaza. But one thing is certain: if I wanted to maintain my own self-respect, I couldn't afford not to pay that cost.

Notes

1 This ground has been covered by D'Souza (1991).
2 See Goffman (1959; 1963).
3 A simplified version of this game is formally analyzed by Crawford and Sobel (1982). Also noteworthy are Austen-Smith (1992) and Bernheim (1994).
4 Goffman's general approach is reflected in the following passage from *The Presentation of Self*: "[Consider] the point of view of the individual who presents himself before [others]. He may wish them to think highly of him, or to think that he thinks highly of them, or to perceive how in fact he feels toward them, or to obtain no clear-cut impression. . . . Regardless of the particular objective which the individual has in mind and of his motive for having this objective, it will be in his interest to control the conduct of the others, especially their responsive treatment of him. This control is achieved largely by

influencing the definition of the situation which the others come to formulate, and he can influence this definition by expressing himself in such a way as to give them the kind of impression that will lead them to act voluntarily in accordance with his own plan" (1959, p. 3).

5 Thus the fact that I use the masculine form of the third-person pronoun (he, him, his) when a gender choice in the singular is unavoidable will not go unnoticed. My declaration here that this choice was made at random and adhered to for consistency's sake will, I fear, avail me little with some readers. This is especially so if the ostentatious display of the feminine pronoun has become a convention among other men writing on these issues.

6 In a lecture, where communication is by spoken word, my options for strategic behavior are greatly expanded. I can use the inflection of my voice, my posture, my gestures, my physical appearance, and some fully chosen words, delivered with mock spontaneity, to manage the impression I convey.

7 For example, many readers are more confident about the accuracy of news reported in a paper whose editorial opinions they share, despite the fact that reporting and editorial functions are strictly segregated at reputable papers.

8 Crawford and Sobel (1982) show that, taking due account of the incentive for strategic expression, more information will be conveyed from sender to

receiver the more similar their views are on how that information should be used.

9 The particular reason for seeking out deviants that is identified here – a desire to avoid being fooled or manipulated in collective deliberations – is not the only motive, and perhaps not even the most important one. Thus Kurtz (1983) suggests other factors that may drive the hunt for heretics. One is a community's need to establish a distinctive identity and to maintain group solidarity: "Group solidarity is seldom strengthened by anything as much as the existence of a common enemy, and the heretic, as a 'deviant insider,' is close at hand" (p. 1085). Another factor is the need of elites to justify their positions in a community: "Through the labeling and suppression of heresy, institutional elites can rally support for their positions through battle with a common enemy" (p. 1087). Howe (1982), in his memoir, recalls how the search for a common enemy led to an obsession with ideological purity among various left-wing political groupings in the 1930s and 1940s: "The political sect has to pin everything on the rightness of doctrine. The party line becomes its most precious good. To call into doubt even an inch of that line is to endanger its survival, so that, in a way, it is quite right to cast out heretics. In a sect, heresy is never incidental" (p. 38). Factors such as these may be at work in the contemporary political correctness movement. However, most of my argu-

ment does not turn on the particular reasons why groups strive to maintain conformity. What matters is that they do so by using the expressive content of political speech to identify deviance.

10 Essential to sustaining this balanced and self-sustaining pattern of inference is the consensus that obtains within a given community that some expressive acts convey non-native as well as literal meanings. That is, receivers know that the sender knows that receivers think that these words are offensive, callous, reactionary, suspicious, indicative of "softness," associated with disloyalty, and so on; it is common knowledge that such speech has negative connotations, even when that is not the sender's literal intent. Thus, when an outsider, through inappropriate use of some loaded terms, makes a *faux pas*, we initially absolve him from any judgment related to values, because we grant that he may not have known the rules. We say, "Perhaps he didn't mean it the way it sounded." His words cannot possibly have the same effective meaning for us when we cannot be sure that he knew how we might interpret them.

11 An excellent analysis of the speech and its reception may be found in Leisi (1989).

12 This is the conclusion of Benjamin Frankel, conveyed to me in personal correspondence. It is consistent with views of the linguist Ernst Leisi, as stated in Leisi (1989).

13 These quotations are taken from an English translation of the speech provided by the German consulate in Boston and entitled "Remembrance speech by Philipp Jenninger, MP, in connection with the pogroms carried out by the Nazi regime against the Jews in Germany 50 years ago."

14 Thus this particular example does not exactly fit the theory sketched in Sections 2 and 3. Some in the audience may have known that Jenninger was no Nazi sympathizer, but thought that he had to be punished for sounding like one, or else the real neo-Nazis would gain authority to speak more freely. This view would explain why Michael Fuerst, deputy chairman of the Jewish Council in Germany, was also forced to resign his position after saying publicly: "I welcome that [Jenninger] described in full clarity what was happening in Germany between 1933 and 1938, especially the fact that everything that Hitler did was strongly supported by the masses of all Germans" (Associated Press 1988). Jenninger's reckless talk was not to be welcomed. That other Germans might begin to speak openly in this way was precisely the problem.

15 The scare quotes are meant to convey the ambiguity implicit in calling the policy "progressive." Whether sanctions would in an objective sense promote progress for South African Blacks was debatable. Yet, once the meaning in effect that embracing sanctions implies siding with South Africa's freedom

fighters was established, to many observers, support for the policy definitely *gave the impression* of being progressive. Thus, in this subjective sense, it was a progressive act.

16 Of course, I do not mean to say that all those who openly opposed divestment were uncommitted. Some prominent voices against the policy – David Riesman, Clark Kerr, and Alan Pifer, for example – had (and still have) solid reputations as liberals. I only claim that open opposition to the policy was more likely to be noticed the further to the right of the political spectrum one moved.

17 In due course, cities and towns across the country enacted their own sanctions policies, refusing to deal with businesses tainted by association with South Africa. Union pension funds developed divestment programs. Companies adhering to the Global Sullivan Principles and providing substantial benefits to Black workers and their families in South Africa eventually found it impossible to justify their presence there.

18 Conveniently, the policy was painless for its American advocates, although it may have been a disaster for some Black South Africans. Nota bene: the logic of my argument also applies to the sanctions debate *within* South Africa.

19 Numerous examples of the potential for harm are provided by Janis (1982) in his classic study.

20 Mindful of my own "Jenninger problem," I hereby declare, for what it may be worth, that this account does not express my personal views but describes the hypothetical views of a typical American from the early Cold War period.

21 Consider the case of Philip Jessup, nominated for a diplomatic post in the 1950s by President Eisenhower, and rejected by the Senate because some years earlier he had attended a conference on whether US–China policy should be reconsidered. Indeed, it took two decades for that policy to be accommodated to reality by the staunch anti-communist Richard Nixon, who had "natural cover" against the claim of deviance.

22 Support for the New Deal was often raised in this context. Consider the comment of Nebraska Senator Hugh Butler about former Secretary of State Dean Acheson, after Acheson publicly supported Alger Hiss: "I watch his smart-aleck manner and his British clothes and that New Dealism, everlasting New Dealism in everything he says and does, and I want to shout, Get out, Get out. You stand for everything that has been wrong with the United States" (quoted in Victor Navasky, 1980, p. 21). Evidently, there was more going on here than just the fight against communism.

23 The 1987 campaign against Robert Bork's nomination to the Supreme Court is a classic case. It was launched by Senator Edward Kennedy with a speech

that described Bork's America as "a land in which women would be forced into back alley abortions, blacks would sit at segregated lunch counters, rogue police could break down citizen doors in midnight raids" (Gest 1987). This gross distortion was part of a calculated rhetorical strategy, which in due course prevailed. The strategy was spelled out with remarkable candor in a memorandum circulated among anti-Bork interest groups: "To offset the White House's emphasis on Bork's intellectual qualifications, opponents need to imprint his non-judicious turn of mind with such labels as: closed minded . . . insensitive, prejudicial . . . injudicious, rigid, cold and indifferent, lacking empathy, flaming and inflexible, insensitive to injustice" (Advocacy Institute, "The Bork Nomination: Seizing the Symbols of the Debate," July 14, 1987, pp. 5–6). I am aware that many readers will object to my mentioning this episode in the context of McCarthyism. But my point is analytical, not political. I mean only to show how the *smear* – defined as the misrepresentation of a political figure's expression so as to cast him in a morally dubious light before the public – is a ubiquitous tactic of partisan politics. Smears of President Clinton's nominees have also occurred. Just after he withdrew the nomination of Lani Guinier to head the Justice Department's Civil Rights Division, an issue of the conservative *American Spectator* appeared, trumpeting the fact that Guinier's father had been close to the Communist Party in the 1940s and 1950s.

24 Orwell (2013, pp. 132–3).

25 It was not always so; witness the limits that many institutions imposed on Jewish enrollments earlier in this century – limits openly justified by a concern about Jewish "overrepresentation." When, in the late 1970s, the applications of Asians to elite colleges and universities began to grow more rapidly than their enrollments, no similar justification of restricting the access of these superbly qualified students could be made. In fact, what appears to have been informal ceilings on Asian admissions was swept away, as complaints about the disparity between the acceptance rates of Asian and White applicants were made public. Indeed, the combination of minority status with outstanding academic performance among Asian Americans has proved profoundly unsettling to the practice of affirmative action in college admissions. See Takagi's (1992) excellent study of these developments.

26 A corporate executive discussing his firm's financial status with both bankers and union leaders present in the room is more credible with each, by virtue of the presence of the other: he wants the bankers to think that the firm is doing well and the union leaders to think that it's doing poorly; and both parties know this! See Farrell and Gibbons (1989). A similar logic constrains the chances of rhetorical

manipulation when a politician commits himself to giving exactly the same speech on racial issues to both a Black and a White audience, as Bill Clinton did during the 1992 presidential campaign.

27 Thus Strauss (1952) argues that, by "writing between the lines," some medieval philosophers engaged in criticism of the status quo without provoking a charge of heresy. They disguised their arguments in such a way that they would not be understood by lay authorities, but could still be grasped by other philosophers: "A man of independent thought can utter his views in . . . print without incurring danger, provided he is capable of writing between the lines. . . . For the influence of persecution on literature is precisely that it compels all writers who hold heterodox views to develop a peculiar technique of writing, the technique which we have in mind when speaking of writing between the lines" (p. 24). Very much in keeping with the spirit of this essay, Strauss goes on to draw implications concerning how these texts should be read – and he draws them from his presumptions about how they were written. His theory of reading rests fundamentally upon the fact that the philosopher speaks to multiple audiences.

28 Not just women but men, too, will apply the stricter rules. Thus a man can be condemned *by other men* for saying something in the presence of women that is commonly said in their absence. Yet it would be a mistake to dismiss this as an unfair "double

standard" because, with a different audience, the same words do not have the same effective meaning.

29 Most "racist" remarks discovered to have been made by public figures have this character. Although this does not excuse the offender, it sharpens our understanding of the offense – which is more often due to naivete than to malice. Yet, because the malign are more likely than the benign to overlook the fact that some expression might offend an unintended listener, calling such gaffes "racist" is consistent with the logic of strategic inference.

30 Discouraging insider criticism can have significant costs, a point explored at length in Hirschman's (1970) important book. Precisely because it is rooted in familiarity with and concern for the group, such criticism can be compelling, but also painful to hear. Yet, when insiders are not permitted to voice their dissatisfactions, they may "exit" – that is, withdraw from active participation in the public life of the group – leaving the discussion to the contented and forestalling needed reform. Hirschman therefore stresses the importance of "loyalty" – a speaker's willingness to stay and argue over how the group should conduct its affairs, even at great personal costs to himself. This is to be distinguished from "blind loyalty" – that reflex and uncritical endorsement of one's communal norms captured in the phrase "my country, right or wrong." The "loyal" political critic in a multiple audience environment

faces the dilemma that, to be effective, his inter-
ventions must be articulated publicly and heard by
friends and enemies alike. Walzer (1988) describes
this dilemma in his wise and elegant study of social
criticism: "Intimate criticism is a common feature
of our private lives; it has its own (implicit) rules.
We don't criticize our children, for example, in
front of other people, but only when we are alone
with them. The social critic has the same impulse,
especially when his own people are confronted by
hostile forces. . . . But the social critic can never be
alone with his people; there is no social space that is
like familial space, and so the critic's intimacy can't
take the form of private speech; it can only shape
and control his public speech. A certain forbearance
qualifies or alternates with his stringency. He must
speak, however, and speak out loud so long as there
is any hope that he will be listened to among his own
people. . . . The silence of the connected social critic
is a grim sign – a sign of defeat, a sign of endings"
(pp. 151–2).

31 Thus conservative Supreme Court Justice Clarence
Thomas was described by a (Black) legal scholar
critical of his nomination as "black on the outside,
but white on the inside" (see Carter 1991, p. 33).
And William Lucas, a Republican gubernatorial
candidate, was savaged by a Black member of the US
House of Representatives, who said: "Biologically he
is black, but he is not black in the spirit of Martin

Luther King or the Civil Rights Movement." Carter (1991) discusses with insight some of the problems with the notion of racial authenticity that are implicit in these remarks (see Loury 1986).

32 That the desire to avoid offending communal norms has shaped the doing of science is a basic theme in the sociology of knowledge, as developed for example in Kuhn (1962).

33 Coleman (1989, pp. 76–8). Some years later, when lecturing on their important treatise *Crime and Human Nature* in the shadow of Harvard University, Richard Herrnstein and James Q. Wilson (1985) were drowned out by students chanting, "'Wilson, Herrnstein, you can't hide. You believe in genocide!'"

References

Associated Press. 1988. Kristallnacht flap spurs 2d resignation. *Chicago Tribune*, November 17, p. 12.

Austen-Smith, David. 1992. Strategic models of talk in political decision making. *International Political Science Review* 13(1): 45–58.

Bernheim, B. Douglas 1994. A theory of conformity. *Journal of Political Economy* 102(5): 841–77.

Carter, Stephen. 1991. *Reflections of an affirmative action baby*. New York: Basic Books.

Coleman, James, S. 1989. Response to the Sociology of Education Award. *Academic Questions* 2(3): 76–8.

Crawford, Vincent and Joel Sobel. 1982. Strategic information transmission. *Econometrica* 50: 1431–51.

D'Souza, Dinesh. 1991. *Illiberal education*. New York: Free Press.

Farrell, Joseph and Robert Gibbons. 1989. Cheap talk with two audiences. *American Economic Review* 79(5): 1214–23.

Gest, Ted. 1987. Reagan's choice to shape the supreme court: A new majority moves to the right. US News and World Report, July 13, p. 28.

Goffman, Erving. 1959. *The presentation of self in everyday life*. New York: Anchor Books.

Goffman, Erving. 1963. *Stigma: Notes on the management of spoiled identity*. New York: Simon & Schuster.

Herrnstein, Richard, and James Q. Wilson. 1985. *Crime and human nature*. New York: Simon & Schuster.

Hirschman, Albert. 1970. *Exit, voice, and loyalty*. Cambridge, MA: Harvard University Press.

Howe, Irving. 1982. *A margin of hope: An intellectual autobiography*. New York: Harcourt Brace Jovanovich.

Janis, Irving. 1982. *Groupthink: Psychological studies of policy decisions and fiascoes* (2nd edn). Boston, MA: Houghton Mifflin.

Keane, John, ed. 1985. *The power of the powerless*. Armonk, NY: M. E. Sharpe.

Kuhn, Thomas. 1962. *The structure of scientific revolutions*. Chicago, IL: University of Chicago Press.

Kurtz, Lester. 1983. The politics of heresy. *American Journal of Sociology* 88(6): 1085–115.

Leisi, Ernst. 1989. Der Mißerfolg von Philipp Jenningers Rede. *Neue Zürcher Zeitung*, January 12.

Loury, Glenn. 1986. John Conyers and the new McCarthyism. *Detroit News*, October 19.

Navasky, Victor. 1980. *Naming names*. New York: Viking Press.

Orwell, George. 1968. *In front of your nose, 1945–1950*, vol. 4 of *The collected essays, journalism and letters of George Orwell*. New York: Harcourt, Brace & World.

Orwell, George. 2013. *Politics and the English language*. London: Penguin.

Revel, Jean-François. 1983. *How democracies perish*. New York: Harper & Row.

Sagarin, Edward, ed. 1980. *Taboos in criminology*. Beverly Hills, CA: SAGE.

Strauss, Leo. 1952. *Persecution and the art of writing*. Glencoe, IL: Free Press.

Takagi, Dana. 1992. *The retreat from race*. New Brunswick, NJ: Rutgers University Press.

Walzer, Michael. 1988. *The company of critics*. New York: Basic Books.

12 301